BODY MEMORY

Meriwether Clarke

Attention schools and businesses: for discounted copies on large
orders, please contact the publisher directly.

For information contact:
Unsolicited Press
Portland, Oregon
www.unsolicitedpress.com
orders@unsolicitedpress.com
619-354-8005

Book Design: Kathryn Gerhardt
Editor: Summer Stewart
ISBN: 978-1-963115-62-8

Contents

"All water has a perfect memory and is forever trying to get back to where it was."

Toni Morrison, "The Site of Memory"

SEPTEMBER

It's early autumn morning. Two swallows
fight for sound and space.

By afternoon hawks will circle
and no one will want

to sit outside. Fencing splits

the field in half. Crickets and
cicadas sing. I miss

the city, unexpectedly. There is so little
space there, but

so much to see

and all my friends
who once lived so close.

I think of them

as a child remembers
learning to walk.

      Do children recall such things?
After all,

the body moves before

it learns to speak. And without
words what can there

be of memory, without memory
what can there be

of days?

I.

ORANGES

Once, it was hard to
pass Mimi's orange tree and not
pick its heavy boughs clean.

My parents said I had to eat
what I took. But I did not like oranges, their pulpy,
sometimes chewy, texture. I did not like

their skin, my hands always failures at maintaining
a circular curve as I opened
it up. All I loved were my fingertips.

With an orange beneath them they became sweet,
scented and luxurious, as I sat before
the broken TV in her living room.

There was no one there to listen as I hummed
to myself and stared at the blank, black screen.
Out the window, the tree slapped itself

in wind. My chest still looked flat and I
wondered what would hurt when it began
to rise. My fingers were sticky

and I remembered the peel in tatters
on the floor, the fruit in my hands
dented and, just now, leaking.

PRAYER

He sees everything,
        they reminded us
in Catholic School. He sees

the inside of your desk,
        your mouth
when you chew, your body

under blankets. He doesn't sleep

because in heaven
        day and night
don't need

to exist. There is light, but no
        sun, garlands
of stars,

but no dark sky
        to pin
them to. As a child,

I always drew
        during Church. I sketched
rows of women while the Priest

spoke. They all

had big, soft eyes.
        Some were tall,
some with hair

to hide behind. Their dresses
        touched the
ground—the place

where bare feet kissed an earth
        that looked back up
all the way from the porch

to the edge
        of the hem-deep river.

HAIRLESS AND CLEAN

Baby leg hairs stand
up straight. They are new
and shave off easily, covered in

bright pink gel that
thickens into cream when
rubbed between palms.

Water falls and rivulets form
until my calf is caged
in white foam. It is

beautiful, but I don't want
to draw blood, so I
slather more on and sweat

in the steam and think of
caterpillars turning to liquid
in cotton wombs. How strange

it must be,
melting into something
else, entirely.

SOME LITTLE GIRLS

are expendable, it seemed to me,
        five years old and lying in bed
as my father closed my window. A week before,

a preteen in Tulsa was lured out
        of a slumber party by a strange
man, stolen and strangled. I barely knew

what the second word mean, *strangle,* but
        felt it in my throat,
like swallowing a piece of rope,

as I said it out loud. Only a year later,
        JonBenét disappeared. Her face
on the cover of *People Magazine* was

that of a small woman's, crowned
        in golden hair. *Like a cherub,* the lady
in the checkout line said.

Horrible, my mother replied covering
        my ears. My lips were not
her lips, so perhaps I was safe.

Perhaps only angels are destined
            to die, I thought, searching
my back for something like

the bud of wings.

TO HOLD

At the museum I count
the number of times the Virgin Mary

went to heaven. In almost all,
her palms are straight and

tightly clasped as she
ascends. Later versions give

more warmth to her serenity— face
rounder but still placid as

a drying lake. Only one image
is dedicated to her birth. I stand

before it, my fingers unsure

what to do in a room
of so much not to touch.

Little Mary lays in a nurse
maid's arms. The most I can see

is the crest of her head,

even then, awaiting
its halo. Her mother

lies exhausted on the bed,
her hands more

limp and downcast than her

eyes as if she was tired, already,
from knowing what she bore

was not hers at all.

BLUE

I try to tell
my loved ones of the way it tastes:

harsh, first, and then, sometimes,

a sweetness—

Water hiding

Cousin J's feet
as he smiles like a
little prince.

Mama in the RV, watching

out the window. M and I

pretending to be mermaids.

This is how we learned
the value of long braids,

something to wrap around
our necks when quiet

blooms into silence. Evenings are fish fry
       dinners, whiskey hidden

in tabasco bottles while

no one says
what they really think. Instead, they discuss

the splendor
       of nature. How beautiful the trees are,
someone says. How

peaceful the water. I remember it
sloshing in my mouth.

Cold teeth clack and I
       try not to swallow
try not
       to spit it out.

RUG BURN

I was twelve and sitting in a bookstore basement.
The Lady and the Unicorn lay open
on the floor. I don't remember what

I was wearing and it doesn't matter—which is,
to say, regardless of my young chest
hanging out, it was still mine. He must have seen

the way my eyes were clouded by words.
He must have liked my legs tucked under
my chin, the split

open peach of me. Bridges of skin
and bone swerved over my pit.
I coated myself

with a smile. Before I could say *hello* he was
beside me, arm on my shoulders, hand
dangling near my breasts.

I hid my palms and thought of lights
on a Christmas tree— stars
near enough earth to extinguish.

SIPHON

I would like my body
to be
less intrusive, less
protruding. I
would like to fit into
the cast
of a body smooth and lithe,
able to flatten
against walls and slide
under doors.
I would like to sleep on the ground
and be
barely seen, peel
myself up
in the morning and walk
like a shadow: all
edges, all length, throughout
all the day.
The floor would
never crack beneath me, chairs
would never
sag. *How light* the wind
would think,
pushing me along. I would be like
girls from the magazines where the
models are

so thin. Their pictures make me wish
I could
sink into myself the way
they sink
into themselves, the
way the ground
in Arizona sinks into
itself
when water is taken
from beneath it
and it becomes concave
and houses fall
and then there is
nothing left.

COTTONWOOD

On my thirteenth birthday I became
a cottonwood tree.

It was painless and fast, the soft dough
of bones rising before

silence as the day moved on.
The other saplings

welcomed me, whispered
what's it like

to move? They told me they wished to run--
in thunderstorms and in

fire season, at the occasional pinch
of pocket knives

carving lopsided hearts into
their feet.

READING VOGUE IN THE BATH

I was once a girl in the bath.
In the bath a girl learns about her body.
Being a girl is all about learning how

to be a girl. I read an article
about a man who said he only noticed
former girlfriend's

physical flaws

because of constant
self-criticism.
Another thing to keep quiet,

I noted. I smiled and
edged the magazine into water. I tried
to imagine what it meant for love

to be made
and all these women —*gorgeous women*—
complaining about cellulite   bloated stomachs   ugly

feet.

I felt bad for them but I
adored the man. He was so generous
to try and convince them they

were beautiful and I wished,
so badly,
he would do the same for me.

FIRST

Bell-leaves out the window ring.
        There, just beyond them, is
where we met.

You crowned me with dandelions,
        blew on my face, tried to
pluck out my hair

strand by strand. *What am I?*
        Made of grass? I said. It
should have been a sign

you were unkind
        when you nodded *yes* and asked me
to lay down. Blades beneath me

folded into a nest, a pyre.
        You told me I was
the Virgin Mary, a body

in a halo, gold and white.
        Your mouth was birds
pecking grain. My belly

was open now, stretching

      as fingers unfurl

after making a fist.

WOMEN AS COWS

When I expand,
let it be horizontally
forward, pushing me on
my hands and knees. Let
my breasts morph into one
mottled half-sphere, hanging
in a balloon below my
belly. Let me learn
to love the taste of grass, blades
disintegrating on
my tongue
in a sour lime-green
swill. Let my father learn
to count on me for milk.
Let my mother give up dreams
of a small pink baby
and learn I am now
a pile of bones stuffed into
the shape of a cow,
no longer uncertain
of my purpose.

BODY OF WATER

At night
my skin began to
change. It was something new

to cry about:
first, the disappearance
of birds outside

and then lines
where my body
morphed into little slopes

covered in half-buried
worms. Sometimes
I asked the mirror

why I looked this way.
I wanted
my sister's hands. I wanted

legs like a doll. At the very least,
I wanted a return
to my old

girl-shape: feathery and lean, durable

as plastic, now bent
in too many
ways to recognize myself.

In bed I closed my eyes
and pretended
my hands

were pieces of paper

thrown out the window and scattered
below. My body became a pond,
fluid and skinless.

I was something with distance
from land, something more
than flesh for blood

to bloom out of, like the scent
of a petal   fragrant and
mostly unseen.

II.

WAYS WE ARE TAUGHT

Forty minutes ago, we first met. Ten minutes
after that,

I told him about the woman I met in Amsterdam
who told me

she was dying. Now we stand by a lake and he fingers
my back.

If I had more hands they'd lift my hands to
push his

away. If I were shoulder-less, when he turns me to
face him

there would be nothing left for him to grab. But I am just
ten fingers, ten toes,

one neck, and one sloping spine— *a perfect body*, he says,
leaning in

for a kiss. I can't help but want to laugh, and do
until my teeth

relax into a grin and we continue
our walk.

RUNAWAY

A painting
of my mother hangs in the dining room. She waits

all day
for me to come in. I watch her

watch me eat
each meal, her face frozen at twenty-two,

mine older
every second. At night, I walk to the crossroad

where I saw
her last. *Don't shout, don't follow,* I say aloud,

imitating her
gravel voice. It is only then

that I remember how
she once looked: grey and solemn, walking toward

woods filled
with cabins she said were charnel houses

and rivers

she promised would someday flood into lakes.

STASIS

My no is a question
I want to yell. My no
is two letters that

bloom into
cries when
you see me there and stare

without saying hello. I feel
as used as a bed spring. As a teenager,
my heart broke almost

every day.

Sometimes I imagined
cutting off my hands
on the way to piano lessons.

Early Dylan
looped in my head. I sang
Sad-Eyed Lady of the Lowlands

in the mirror and wished my eyes were also a
a place where the moonlight

could swim. At school
I watched popular boys yell and wondered
what sorrow it would take

for them to re-learn silence.

CRUSH

I've never imagined the color
of my lungs.

They live inside me, hidden so well
as to daily forget

the miracle of breathing.

Instead, I dream of your face.
Like any desperate,

almost-lover, I convince myself I own it, a little.
The sound

of your voice becomes a scent to inhale and
circulate beneath

my skin like blood. As if my blood is not
enough. Because

it's not, these days or any,
unless a man

says *hello,* or someone
asks

to take my picture. You will never do these things
to me,

or other things, and this I know
but refuse

to admit. Instead I tell myself everything
inside me

is flawed and this is why
I'm so sad.

I tell myself my irises are selfish, my hips too
hungry, my clavicle

too tired to flap its wings.

MY DRESS

covers
skin covers creases and
curves no one

knows exist drapes
at my waist

falls to the
ground and sweeps

over my knees   like a curtain

In this field   am I light does

the sun make me glow

is this

how bulbs feel beneath
lampshades

Hot and unsure
how to be turned off

but wanting it wanting
       the moths to stop

circling stop

butting their heads
       into this heat

that is not theirs?

GUEST

In the shower I hope
to fall

like a city:

white marble returned to
just another

hard and crooked
stone.

Currents do not soften
me.

Instead cracks become doors,
open and

hingeless. The rooms of my
neck and hips

are now as small and un-
attached as submarines

and, in this way, I'll float
before I sink.

EARLY DEPICTION OF A PASSION I UNDERSTOOD

Marianne Dashwood, wandering in the rain.
Marianne Dashwood, who, earlier in the
film, twisted her ankle
chasing blue sky, returns to her
cave, a wetness.

IF I WERE THIN

I would sleep
on frozen rivers and wake up
breathing smoke. The tips
of my fingers would show
their bones and when
I tap them
it wouldn't be a way
to sing. With a face no longer
a crown I could cut
off my lips and still be pretty.

In the world that's real
even my throat
is an anomaly: some days
a water spout and others, just
the fitting of a pipe.

MEATLOCKER

Where he takes me,
hand-in-hand. What I see is wrinkles
in his suit, two cases of wine by the door,
bags of fertilizer the gardeners use

to plant hydrangeas. We look for beer, laugh
when we open the freezer and see stacks of
beef in white paper, cuts scrawled in black.

It's funny when I grab
tenderloin and hand it to him, let him
lean in and kiss me,
stiffen, but don't move,

when he pushes the solid rock of meat
against my breast. It is cold like outside, it is not
his hand reaching into

my chest, past the skin,
past the sternum, it is not
his hand and I am   oh
          so grateful for that.

STOMACH

The boats
that moor here
are pills: stop bleeding, make
happiness, calm down.
The shore is

a pair of hands pushed
into a crooked
ring. It was a sunny
day and how dust
still lingers, so like
the impulse, always,

    to shrink.

DESIRE

One hundred six outside
      and the fire escape
is the coolest place.

I can see
      the city lights from here, so
sharp and precious I'm certain

wanting them
      will bring me harm.
I stay still instead and think

of what else I know
      with certainty. Here
is one thing: my body is a panther

chasing its tail. Here is
      another: my body is not
a bird's. I look down anyway

and can't hold back
      the wish to fly some place far,
where no one dies

from not being touched.

CUP OVERFLOWS

I used to think love
meant wanting to be

a seed in the rot
of a tree—not
the kind that falls and becomes

careworn and
         wood spent;

that blooms its own
creekside haven
or place to keep

a leaning shoulder.
The kind that remembers
how fire glows and tries

to replicate it—   be steam
be flame   be always there,
unexiting and uninvisible.

The kind
that is me when I
hold myself

like a broom and wonder

what greatness is not
a little

like mourning?

MY PLANTS ENJOY THE SOLAR ECLIPSE

They have no retinas to burn or
        eyesight to lose. Underneath
the ground they taste soil instead

of looking up. Sometimes,
        it's so hot here
the wind disappears mid-flight.

Bare feet cackle on the baked
        sidewalk. The mountains
hold candles in chains. I pull

burnt leaves off
        the tomato vine and it feels
as if the whole world

is watching.

STARES CAN

invade

like trying to see
      the stems of flowers
through

their vase:
      sunflower, thick and ridged; pansy,
emaciated waif. It makes

me want
      to be bagged, be square-shaped
with a covered neck and

eyes sewn shut.
      Too close to a
shroud, I can't help

but think. And what
      of ice cold tiles on bare pink
feet— oh, how I would

      miss all that.

HEART

First awakened
by wings on the edge
of the sternum, now
poised

for constant flight.
Some days it jumps
to the soles
of my feet, some days

it flies out of my chest and

lands in a nearby parking lot. Some
days it doesn't
come back
at all. Those moments
aren't that empty, in the end.

They are the ocean
after a hurricane: quiet
water reclaiming space
where houses used to be.

COFFEE SHOP BOYS

This one has a wife, I think.

But he touches my hand,
sometimes,
when he gives me change.
My name
on his lips
is an invitation
to a place where doors
all open
with the brush of a thumb.
His eyes are string lights
in a jar. The wires tangle and knot
when I walk by, erupt
in golden blooms
that smell

of burnt milk.
All I see are
daffodils.
Each night, at home,
I imagine
coming across him in the garden.
He thinks
it is mine and chooses to stay,
even when I admit

we have
no water.

SNOWSTORM

While you drew
snowflakes on my ribs

I imagined the felt-tipped
pen was

something real,

      a permanent ice
bonded to skin

that before you was untouched.
It was
      so soft,

like fingers, almost, or lips
small enough to kiss

      each lonely cell.

It was light enough, too, not to last.
      The next day,

shower water became grey
and

I felt

like springtime ground,

sad and bare
in all

this newness.

BOYFRIEND, MAKE BELIEVE

Our hands are leaves
grasping skin,
not pavement.

Our nails are sugared praline

shells, our padded palms
the meat
of the nut, it's back

a curve.

There is love and then
there is
this thing that
makes a day
not time but a way
to stay warm inside

and eat. Downtown windows
are closed eye lids.
I want to be seen and
I want
       to be touched.

In my mind, we lie
beneath a blanket.
The shades are drawn.
The ceiling is train calls and
park grass and

every day
I fall asleep.

EMPTY SPACES

Under the bed.
Inside the hollow legs
of a bamboo chair.
An *O* made by arching
a finger and
a thumb.
Beneath the lid
of the washing machine.
The insides of light
bulbs, even when
they're on. Electricity is
too weightless to count.
Like a prayer
it doesn't
fill its encasement,
only
warms it.

IF WALLS COULD TALK

They would stretch the corners
of their mouths with words like
somnambulism, sentry. They would

click their mossy teeth
until the door remains shut.
In my sleep I would hear

pardons to the flowers enclosed
in a vase, willful enough to
die. It would be childhood,

only sadder. No sister to
climb beside my pillow
and tuck her feet beneath

my weight. No commas in
her breath as she stops
to tell me some small

joy, pockets of fire
now put out.

EARS

Little caves open wide
to catch it all:

cars louder than birds
quieter than the sound

of a saw
trimming trees across

the street. It's hard
to think

with so much noise. Harder
when it's quiet enough

to hear spring
thaw outside.

Daydreams, then,
become edges

of things: dried waterfalls,
stalactites broken

at their roots.

III.

BODY MEMORY

In the dream we're on
a bed together, close, but still,

with air between us.
For once you don't want more
than skin against skin,

more than your chest
seeping into my back.

I'm in the body I had
when I was ten,
the year before men started honking

and Joe at the corner store
told me I'd develop, soon enough.

I wonder if, to you,
I'm the same as always.
As if the woman you love

is really a girl
with a round moon-face

and hair she doesn't know
what to do with.

I could cry (if I were awake)

seeing myself there, so small.
What I always wanted,

what I didn't know I once had--
to be inconsequentially lovely;
an ephemeral light

that no one sees until
it's entirely gone.

SHUT-IN

And in this way
I entered heaven by myself,

imagining no one ever
asked *where's your date?* or

commented on
my breasts again.

It does not feel
human to be watched so much

Or,
it does feel human, it does not

feel fair. Nothing's really fair,

my mother always
says. I think

in another life she was
a philosopher or an artist.

In this one, she owns the most
beautiful store.

She says she keeps it open
to make others happy.

When I tell some people this
they laugh: women

and their *things*—
embroidered linen,

canapé plates, all
frivolities. I say:

these are essentials, not just
pleasures. They are no different from

the feathers birds line their nests with:
something enough

to dull the loneliness
of locking the door

after landing.

FOLLOW THE LEADER

Someone once told me girls
who develop too soon are like dolphins—
always wet and speaking in tongues
no one understands. Their breasts

learn early, though, they are not
like fins. There is no underwater
flight for things the shape of little earths.
There is only digging by mouths

that smell of damp grass
and water that makes you float
face down. It's no surprise it's hard
to trust men who want

to touch me. In dreams, I burn comic books and
renaissance paintings, anything with women
the shape of finely-tuned guitars. In real life
I lunge across my bedroom to tighten

my thighs. I trace figure eights
on car windows. I wear
braids coiled
around a milk-clear gaze.

SELF STORAGE

In what room can I learn
to stand and

dream at once? Of verdancy, of teeth like crystals, of hands
and pens—

These hopes teach me only
one thing:

desire is wanting
two selves at once.

CONSIDER MY MOUTH

The last man I kissed
I met at a bar.

He said I had beautiful
lips and began to rub

my neck. It was tender at first,
then turned to great heaves

of pressure, as if he was trying to
push something he didn't want

to hear out.

HOUSE GHOST

I step into her like a spilled glass of water.
With all

the doors closed, she is shimmering and fine.
There is enough

coolness on my bare pink feet to recall
swimming, the smell

of sunscreen and the sometimes wish to disappear.
In late afternoon

the waves are so dark and fierce I can pretend my limbs
have washed away.

Except for the throb to not quite die, there is nothing
keeping me alive. I become

tissue-thin, like light in the entryway,
seams of dampness

reaching toward
        the ceiling.

CONTUSIONS

after Lucie Brock-Broido

If I lie on my side
crying builds a room.

This is my fifteenth year of
being sixteen.

The walls are still unfinished.
I know I should

stop
writing these poems but

something clicks
in me each time I remember

how deer freeze
when a hunter

and his weapon are near.

HOW TO BE HAPPY

Watch bees closely. See how they always have
so many to come home to.
Imitate that hunt for sweetness, that purposeful flight,

but sing, don't buzz.
       Wear your ankles like a swan's neck.
Forget hurtful things that people say.
Stop imagining your face

is a bruised piece of fruit, is a piece
of fruit
       at all.
Let someone touch you

      to make things better.

Wear a veil on your wedding day
       Have
            a wedding day. No longer
gaze at roadside motels and wish

you could live there. Roll the windows up and remind
yourself that

          even there   you'd be somewhere
impossible to run from,

          even there
you'd be here.

SEPTEMBER

In the morning, I eat grapes and
sip black coffee. I want

my arms to be as narrow as
a staircase in a tower.

There is a lot to sit with, here:
namely, is it me

or them who place my limbs
in a small glass jar

and walk away? The future is history,
I once read. And

if that's true, I'll collect stares
like coins until I weigh

three hundred pounds. Again, I'll
sit and try

to cross my legs in a modest way.
Again, I'll avoid doctors,

continue to prefer predicted death by
heart attack to shame.

The truth is, I think I'll outlast
sidewalks, keep bleeding

every month until I'm out
of possibility. Like grass

edging a building, I'll learn to love

kissing stone.

WHERE HAS ALL THE WATER GONE?

Not into the throat of a sparrow
nor under her wings. Not in a jar
on my porch. Not beneath
a rock, there is no coolness
in the ground anymore. No
safety in the thought there is
always something at the end
of digging. Poverty of dust
and poverty of hope.
A creaking like
how winter is remembered. I learn
about storm chasers in a magazine
and now understand
the pleasure of such a
catching.

TO THE BOYS I DIDN'T MARRY

Sometimes I lie awake, afraid it's because
you didn't ask.

What would I
have done if you had turned to me

and said *be, forever, mine*? Would I
still be there,

slinging rocks
into frying pans, turning empty rooms

into a home? You'd think it was magic, but it
would only be love.

Once, you told me *poetry is magic*.

It is, without the memories
thrown

at an empty wall.
It is, until the poem turns toward you.

Then, like the words of so many women,
it becomes

heresy, whiplash,
the voice of someone too small to know

what grownups mean when they talk
over dinner. Don't

misunderstand me.
There isn't a word you've ever said I haven't

once heard, either from another's mouth or from my own.
Some are even

in those lines you think appeared from nowhere,
floated down from the clouds,

as if the making of meaning
ever works that way.

ETYMOLOGIES

It's not
that difficult to

devastate. To confuse with
ameliorate. To suck
on lips
like diamonds.

To choose
love like
choosing bread— soft
and round enough

to squeeze. To evaluate
a voice without
evaluating

words; as if language
has
selective worth—
girl or

woman not enough
but human
maybe is.

LAKE COUNTRY

The house is quiet except for water
collecting in the sink. It is

as easy as breathing — turning
the faucet on and off.

I don't want to go outside today.
Instead, I build lakes in dirty coffee cups, form

snow out of foamy bubbles.
Nothing is cleaned but my hands, more

pink and tender now
than when I woke and thought of

the time we washed my car.
The run-off escaped in little streams to dry-up

somewhere secret and I was
so content, then,

I didn't even think
to wonder where it went.

AT A GAS STATION IN VERMONT WITH MY BEST FRIEND P

We go to buy juice-box wine and
Cheetos made of fire. Their
dust is glitter-light against our
skin. I love

how we laugh down the aisles, wear
beautiful shoes.
Our calves deserve to be kissed
by gorgeous men, but instead

we have fluorescent lights
and each other. Outside
are too many trees to count and a river
we stand in. Shadows of

the question, *what to do next*,
shimmer on the surface until
we break them with
curved and tender feet.

This is the first time
I've ever felt young,
standing inside
a small sea, with someone

who believes me when
I call it a small sea. What I mean,
you know: something to love we
won't try to hold.

SELF-PORTRAIT NO. 50

Like any good daughter

I know to empty my face before coming home.
I take the syrup out of my throat

and replace it with marbles.
From my hands I wash all residue of pollen

and happiness. I will
not be the girl

people say used to be pretty but now
has *gotten big.* The chocolate hidden

in my bedroom will be gone by Spring,
washed down with seltzer water and

nervous laughs.
When I'm old enough

to sing, I'll tell of the trip we took back East.
It was the Fourth

of July. We walked toward the fireworks show
beside a woman who thought I was your wife,

not your child.
As pops filled the air, I could have melted

in your hands
from joy. On the drive out of town

I wondered what about me
looked

so old. But you charmed her,
in the end. You pointed at her baby,

then at me. She used to be
that small, you said.

SOMEDAY

The moon will rot
in a sky
too hot. Arms of stars

will shiver and try to catch
her falling husk. She will
sink down slowly:

a torn sail left
to drown
in water filled with

hungry fish. I will
watch her out the window.
I will lick her dust

off my hair. It will make
me swell, not from a child
but from silence. An

improbable planet
I'll become,
floating and wondering

if I will
disappear next.

NOTES

"Some Little Girls" references the 1996 murder of American child beauty queen JonBenét Ramsey.

The painting that inspired "To Hold" is titled "The Birth of the Virgin" (1627) by Francisco de Zurbarán. It was first admired in its permanent home at the Norton Simon Museum in Pasadena, California.

The poem "Siphon" references the phenomenon known as subsidence, documented by Arizona journalists, as well as the Arizona Geological Survey at the University of Arizona.

"Stasis" references the Bob Dylan song "Sad-Eyed Lady of the Lowlands," off the record *Blonde on Blonde*, side two.

Marianne Dashwood, mentioned in "Early Depiction of a Passion I Understood," is a primary character in Jane Austen's *Sense and Sensibility*. The film mentioned is the 1995 Ang Lee and Emma Thompson adaptation of the novel.

ACKNOWLEDGMENTS

Many thanks to the editors of the following journals where these poems, or versions of them, first appeared:

Prairie Schooner: "To Hold", reprinted in *Poetry Daily*

Tin House, online: "At a Gas Station in Vermont with my Best Friend, P"

Cimarron Review: "My Plants Enjoy the Solar Eclipse"

The Rupture: "House Ghost"

The Journal: "Ways We are Taught"

Gigantic Sequins: "Follow the Leader," Reprinted in *Best New Poets 2019*

Prelude: "Runaway"

Tinderbox Journal: "September" (page 80)

The Watershed Review: "Women as Cows," "First"

Salt Hill: "Meatlocker"

Blueshift Journal: "Lake Country"

A Dozen Nothing: "Stares Can," "Body of Water," "Cottonwood," "Snowstorm"

Juked: "My Dress"

Leveler: "Blue"

Nomadic Press Journal: "Siphon," "Body Memory"

Entropy: "Desire"

I am tremendously thankful to both my teachers and my classmates at Northwestern and UC Irvine, as well as to the Community of Writers, Vermont Studio Center, and the Virginia Center for the Creative Arts. Many thanks to all at Unsolicited Press. With endless gratitude to my family, for their support and love.

About the Author

Meriwether Clarke's poetry has appeared in *Best New Poets,* *Cimarron Review, Colorado Review, Prairie Schooner, Poetry Daily,* *Seneca Review, Sixth Finch, The Rumpus,* and elsewhere. A graduate of UC Irvine's Programs in Writing and Northwestern University, she has been supported by the Vermont Studio Center, the Community of Writers, and the Virginia Center for the Creative Arts. Her chapbook, *twenty-first century woman,* was released by Dancing Girl Press in 2019. She currently lives in Santa Barbara, California.

About the Press

Unsolicited Press is based out of Portland, Oregon and focuses on the works of the unsung and underrepresented. As a womxn-owned, all-volunteer small publisher that doesn't worry about profits as much as championing exceptional literature, we have the privilege of partnering with authors skirting the fringes of the lit world. We've worked with emerging and award-winning authors such as Amy Shimshon-Santo, Brook Bhagat, Elisa Carlsen, Tara Stillions Whitehead, and Anne Leigh Parrish.

Learn more at unsolicitedpress.com. Find us on Instagram, X, Facebook, Pinterest, Bsky, Threads, YouTube, and LinkedIn. Unsolicited Press also writes a snarky newsletter on Substack.

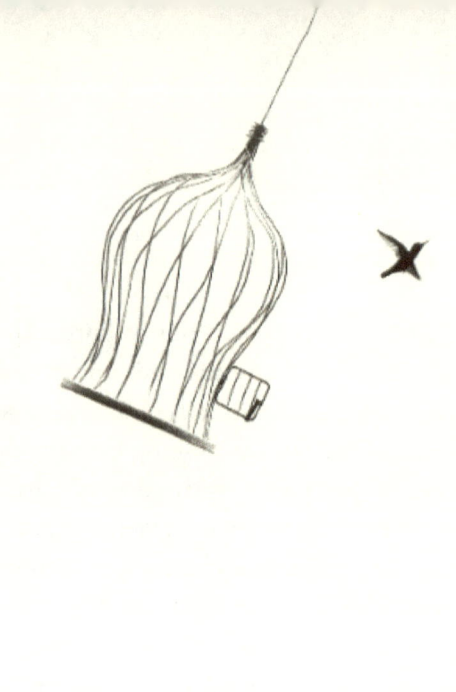

www.ingramcontent.com/pod-product-compliance
Lightning Source LLC
Chambersburg PA
CBHW030458130626
46549CB00007B/2775